Mathematical Dominoes

Book 1

36 blackline masters for 11-14 years

Tracey Macdonald

TarquinGroup
www.tarquingroup.com

Welcome to Mathematical Dominoes 1

Each set of dominoes is in the form of a master that can be photocopied and also provides a chain of answers. Sets need to be prepared in advance as students soon realise that keeping the cards in order as they cut them out means they can avoid attempting all the questions! Students could glue them down on completion so that they can be used as wall displays or 'spot the mistake' activities.

On each domino there is a half that shows an answer and another half with a question. The task is to correctly match up each question and answer in order to get the dominoes to form a continuous loop. Some sets loop clockwise but others go anti-clockwise.

Students can self or peer assess their work to some extent; thus reducing workload for the teacher. With increasing demand to make mathematics more interesting it also provides a fun activity that requires little writing for the students. The students can even be involved in making their own sets which they get to use again, share with other classes or display on the wall. Sets can be scanned into Interactive whiteboard packages so the students can manipulate them on the board as a collective activity or spot deliberate mistakes which you have engineered.

Alternatively, make an extra large set of dominoes and give the students one each. Ask them to create a 'human loop' using their cards. It gets them active and talking about mathematics. For some classes this might mean giving out two different sets and their first task would be to find the people with the other dominoes to make a set with theirs.

Blank domino templates for 12 and 18 domino activities are provided at the end of the book.

Tracey Macdonald

For My Family
Especially Mum, Dad and Kev

Contents

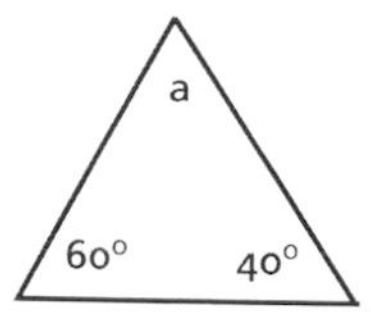

27°

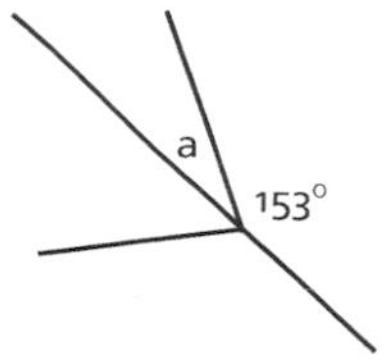

84°

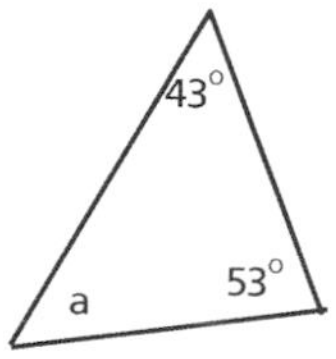

87°

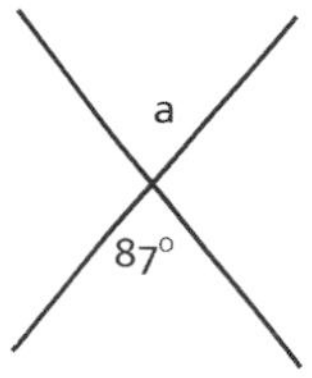

28°

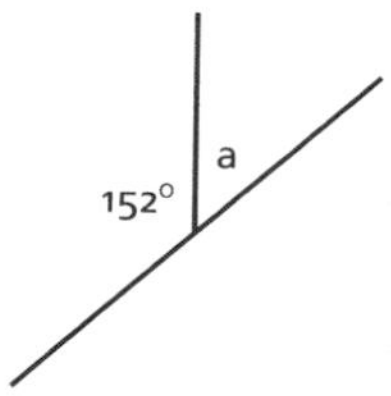

53°

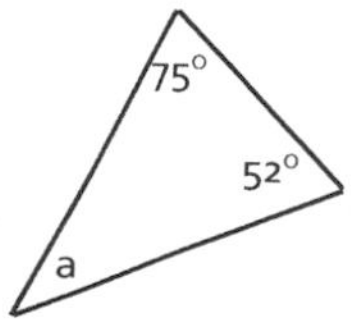

40°

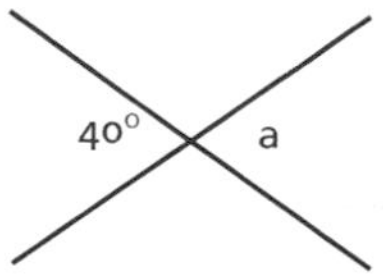

60°

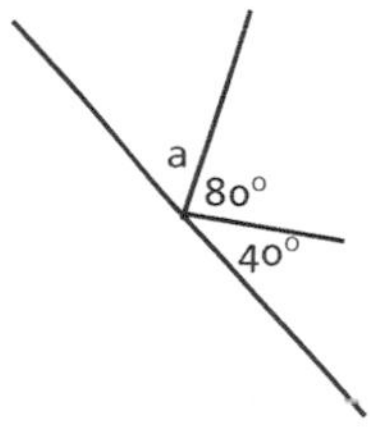

90°

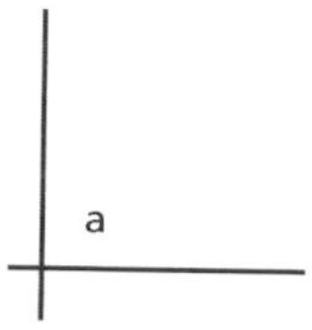

50°

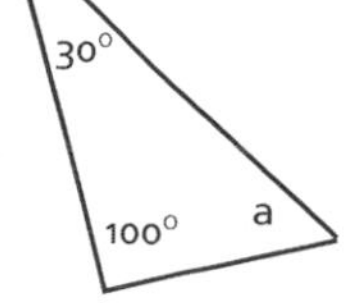

80°

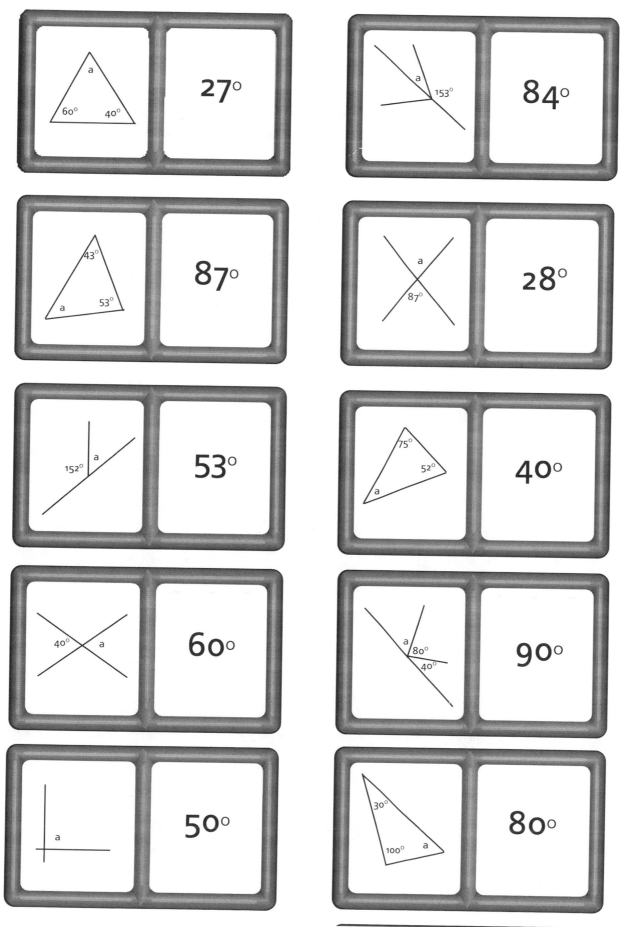

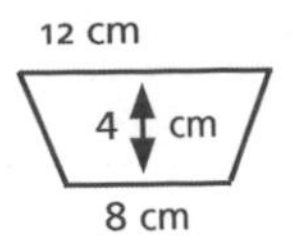

63 cm²

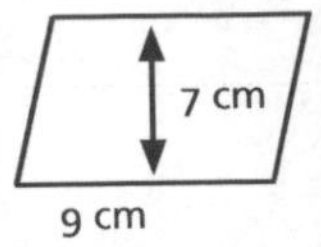

21 cm²

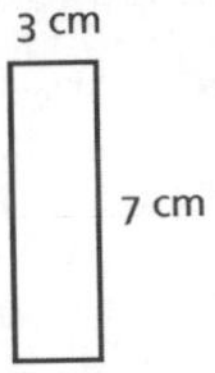

30 cm²

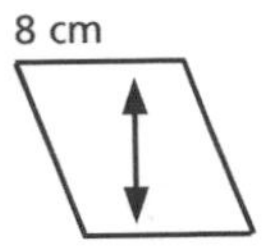

18 cm²

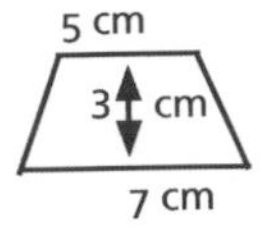

36 cm²

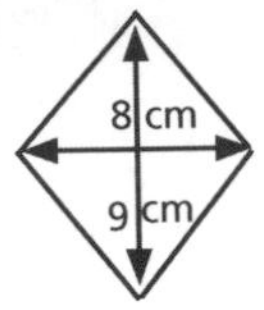

60 cm²

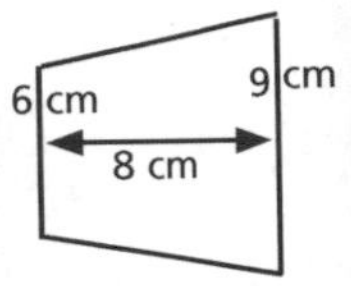

63 cm²

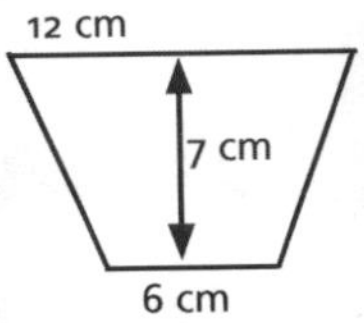

45 cm²

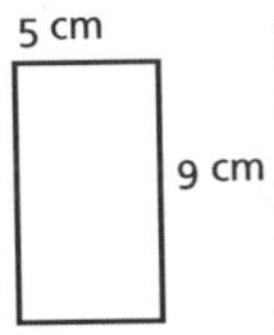

32 cm²

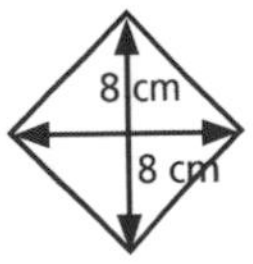

121 cm²

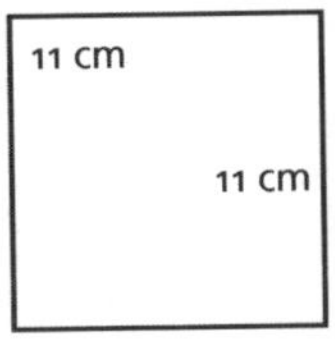

32 cm²

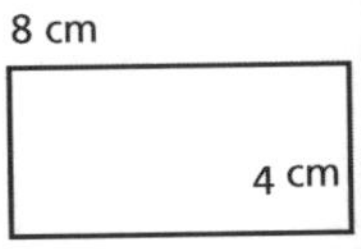

54 cm²

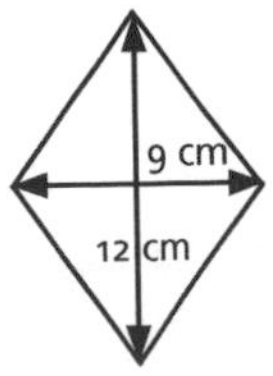

30 cm²

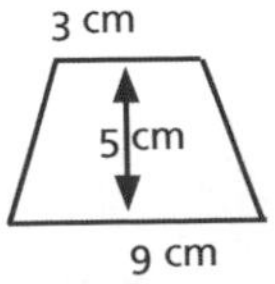

24 cm²

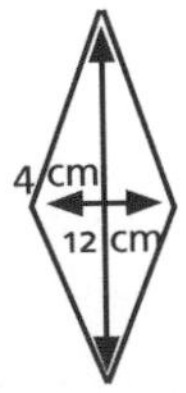

45 cm²

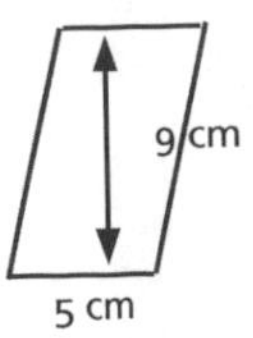

42 cm²

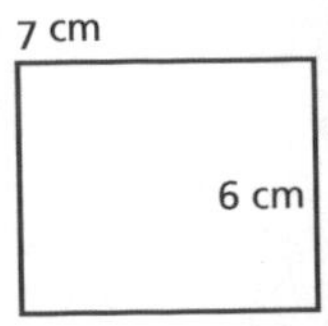

8 cm²

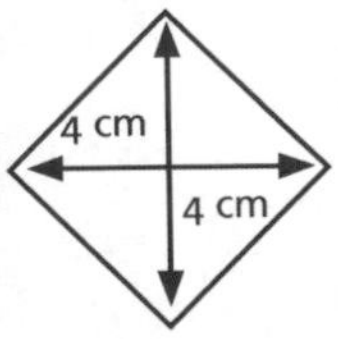

40 cm²

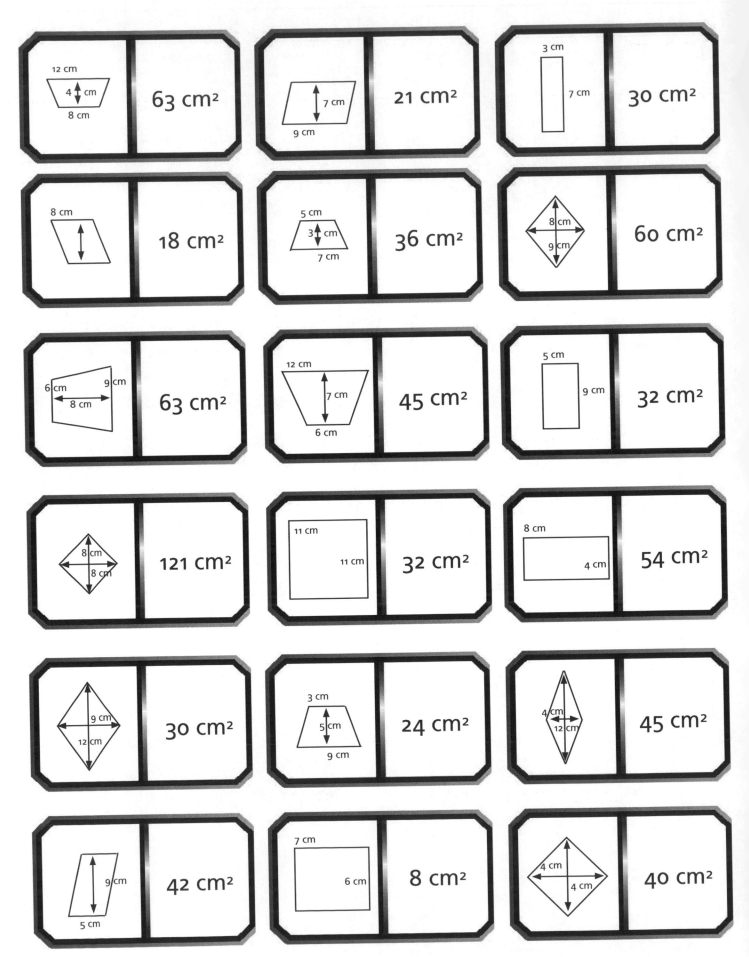

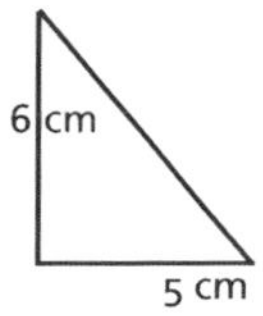

36 cm^2

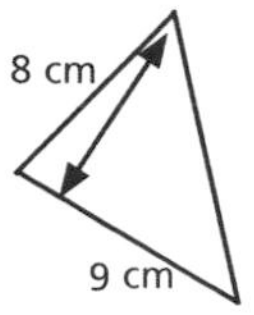

28 cm^2

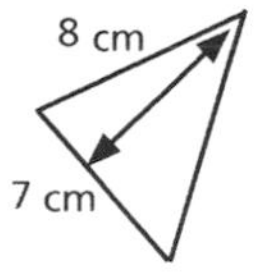

14 cm^2

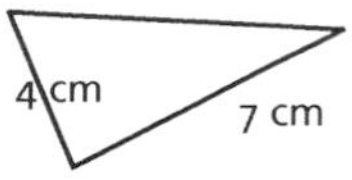

33 cm^2

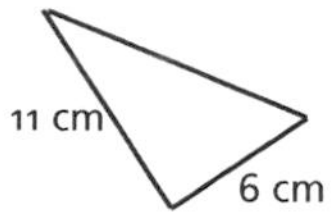

18 cm^2

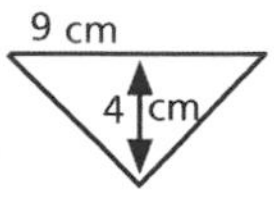

24 cm^2

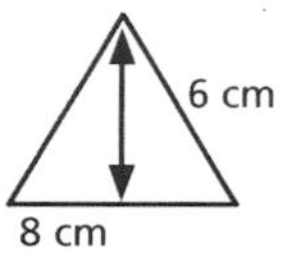

20 cm^2

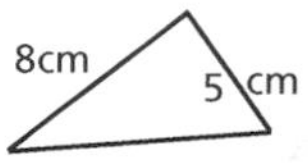

$22\frac{1}{2}$ cm^2

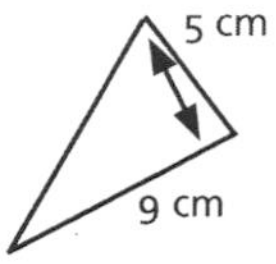

6 cm^2

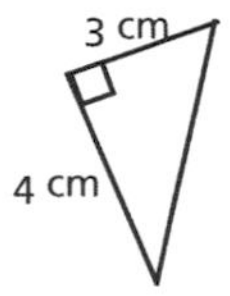

$24\frac{1}{2}$ cm^2

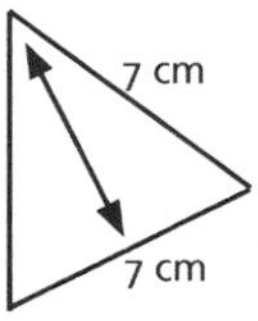

7 cm^2

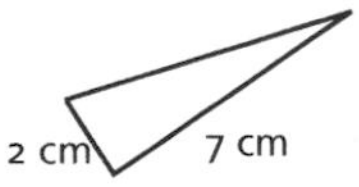

12 cm^2

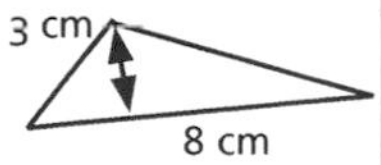

54 cm^2

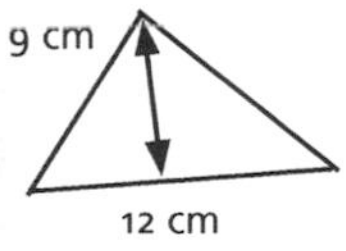

$17\frac{1}{2}$ cm^2

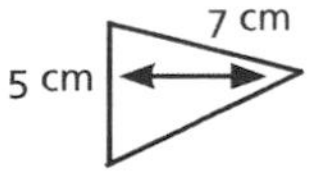

$7\frac{1}{2}$ cm^2

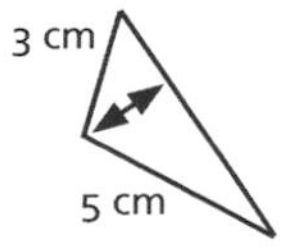

30 cm^2

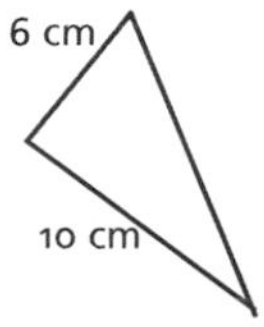

10 cm^2

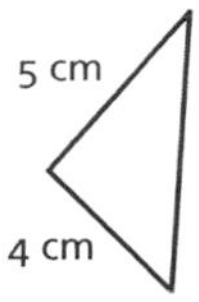

15 cm^2

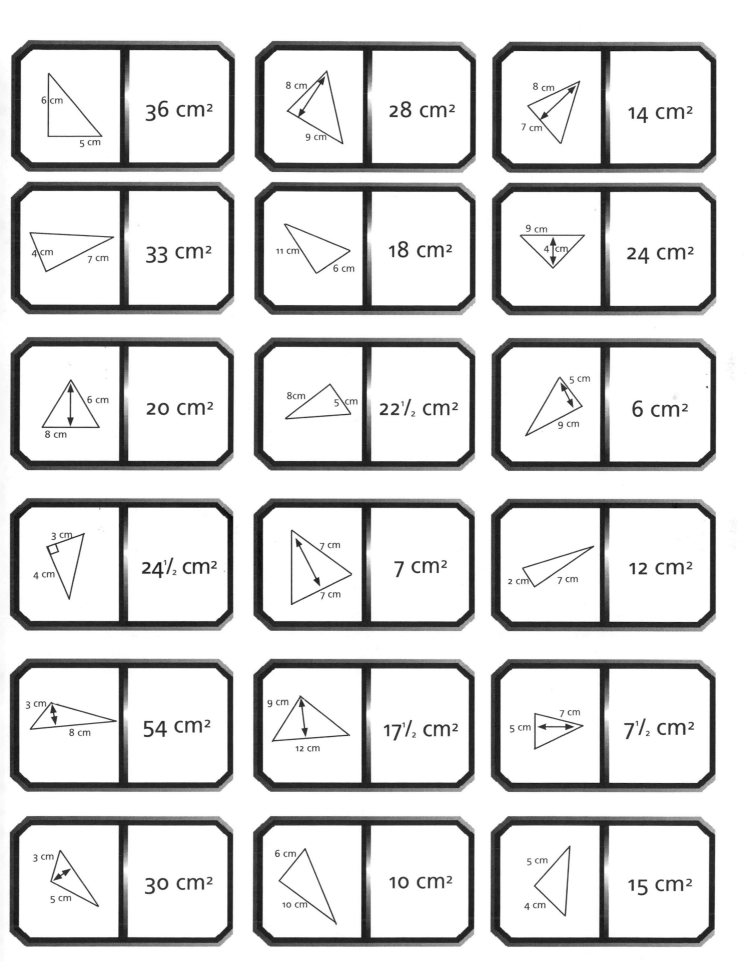

11	Mode of 2, 3, 3, 1, 4, 3, 5, 1
3	Median of 3, 5, 6, 6, 2
5	Range of 8, 3, 3, 9, 4, 3, 5, 2
7	Mean of 2, 2, 1, 2, 1, 3, 3, 2, 2
2	Mode of 5, 6, 3, 2, 4, 7, 6, 1
6	Median of 2, 3, 2, 1, 4, 3, 5, 1
2½	Mean of 8, 3, 2, 1, 4, 3, 5, 6
4	Range of 8, 3, 2, 1, 4, 3, 0, 1
8	Mode of 9, 4, 9, 8, 4, 9, 5, 4
9 and 4	Median of 8, 3, 2, 1, 4, 3, 5, 6, 2, 1
3	Mean of 9, 12, 9, 9, 9, 8, 7
9	Range of 2, 2, 1, 2, 1, 3, 3, 2, 2
2	Mean of 8, 3, 2, 1, 4, 3, 5, 6, 2, 1
3½	Mode of 8, 3, 1, 1, 4, 3, 5, 6, 2, 1
1	Median of 9, 8, 4, 9, 5, 4
6½	Range of 9, 12, 9, 2, 9, 8, 7
10	Mean of 3, 8, 2, 6
4¾	Median of 8, 9, 9, 10, 11, 11, 11, 12, 14

5, 5, 4, 5, 4, 6, 4, ? , 4 Median is 5 Range is 2	4	3, 4, 6, 5, 2, 2, 4, 6, ? Mode is 4	6	8, 3, 1, 9, ?, 6, 5, 2 Median is 5½	15
?, 17, 20, 17, 19, 20, 18 Range is 5	10	?, 3, 2, 1, 4, 3, 5 Mean is 4	6	7, 3, 4, 1, 4, 6, ?, 1, 6 Mode is 6	9
7, ?, 3, 4, 15, 12 Median is 8	4½	2½, ?, 2½, 1, 4½ Mean is 3	13	?, 12, 7, 11, 6, 9, 9, 8, 6 Range is 7 Mean is 9	11
11, 11, ?, 12, 12, 11, 12 Mode is 11	8	6, 8, ?, 6 Median is 7	2	17, 11, ?, 13, 17 Mean is 12 Range is 15	20
12, 11, ?, 11, 11, 11, 12, 19 Range is 9 Median is 11	7	3, 3, 5, 6, 3, ?, 11, 12, 13 Mean is 7	12	9, 9, ?, 10, 11, 11, 11, 12, 14 Mode is 11 Mean is 11	1
?, 2, 1 Median is 1	0	6, 6, 6, ?, 6 Range is 6 Mean is 4.8	3	2, 2, ?, 1, 7, 6, 6, 5, 4 Mean is 4	5

3 + 4 x 2	7
9 - 14 ÷ 7	3
10 - 56 ÷ 8	30
(7 + 8) x 2	1
29 - 4 x 7	47
7 + 8 x 5	18
9 + 36 ÷ 4	32
(9 - 5) x 8	27
(17 - 8) x 3	56
7 x (11 -3)	37
$4 \times 3^2 + 1$	45
5 x (18 - 9)	80
8 x (9 + 1)	44
$2 \times 5^2 - 6$	38
$2 \times (5^2 - 6)$	40
$4 \times (3^2 + 1)$	73
8 x 9 + 1	74
7 x 11 -3	11

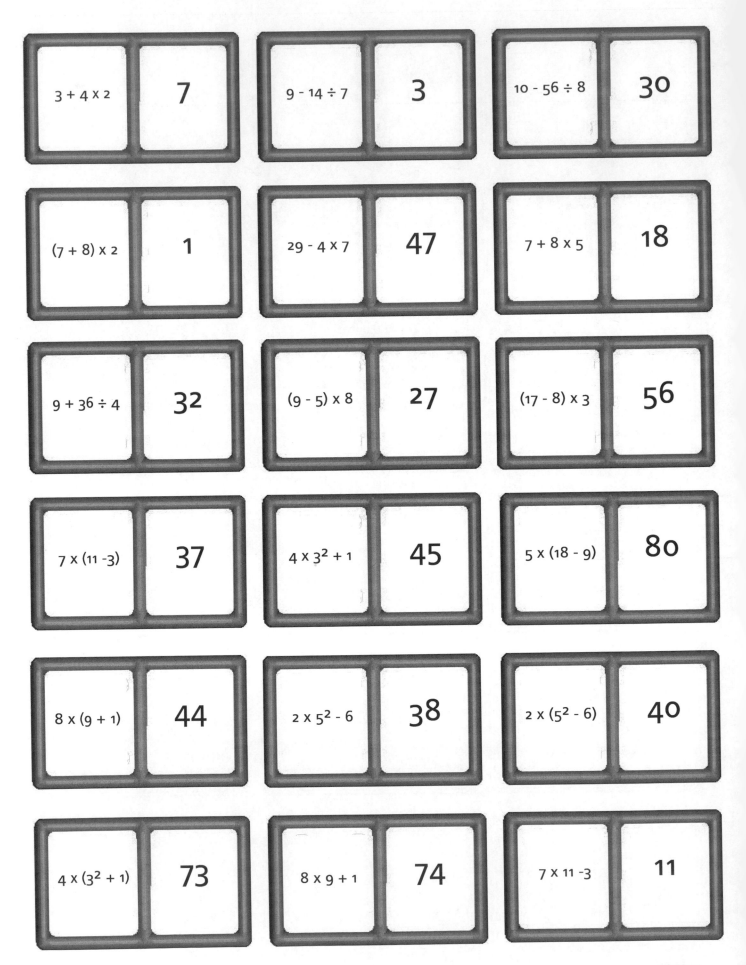

314 cm^2	r = 5 cm, π = 3.14
78.5 cm^2	r = 8 cm, π = 3.14
201 cm^2	d = 12 cm, π = 3.14
113 cm^2	r = 4 m, π = 3.14
50.3 m^2	d = 11 m, π = 3.14
95 m^2	r = 3 mm, π = 3.14
28.3 mm^2	d = 14 mm, π = 3.14
154 mm^2	r = 9 cm, π = 3.14
254 cm^2	d = 10 mm, π = 3.14
78.5 mm^2	d = 12 m, π = 3.14
113 m^2	d = 23 mm, π = 3.14
415 mm^2	r = 2 m, π = 3.14
12.6 m^2	d = 24 m, π = 3.14
452 m^2	r = 15 mm, π = 3.14
706.5 mm^2	d = 15 cm, π = 3.14
177 cm^2	r = 0.5 m, π = 3.14
0.79 m^2	r = 1 cm, π = 3.14
3.14 cm^2	d = 20 cm, π = 3.14

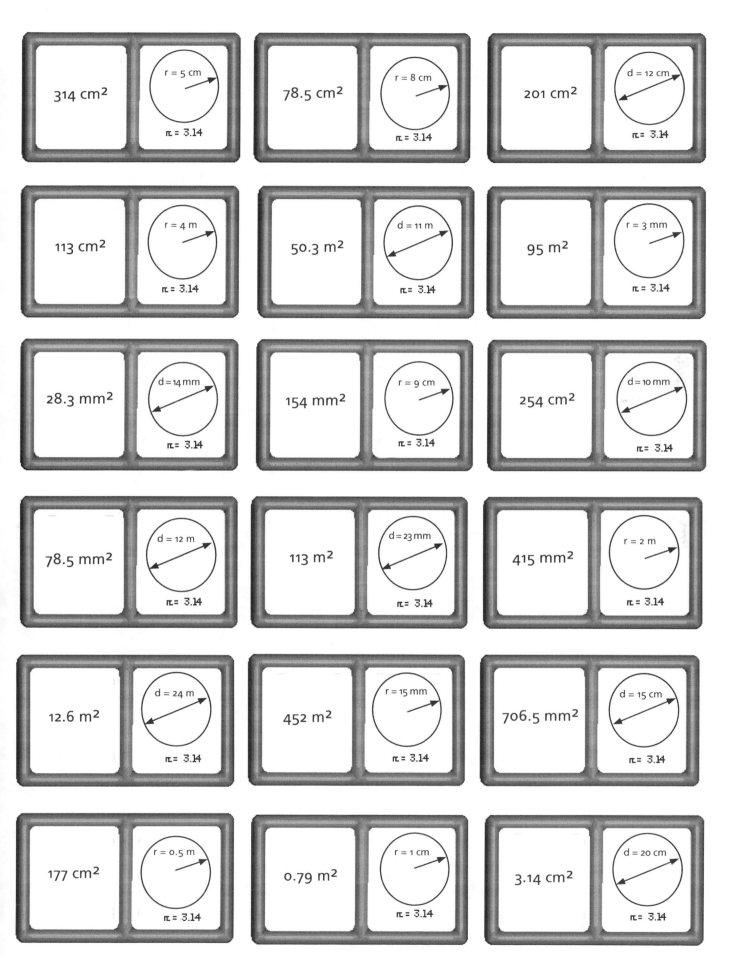

62.8 cm | r = 5 cm, $\pi = 3.14$	31.4 cm | r = 8 cm, $\pi = 3.14$	50.3 cm | d = 12 cm, $\pi = 3.14$
37.7 cm | r = 4 m, $\pi = 3.14$	25.1 m | d = 11 m, $\pi = 3.14$	34.6 m | r = 3 mm, $\pi = 3.14$
18.8 mm | d = 14 mm, $\pi = 3.14$	44 mm | r = 9 cm, $\pi = 3.14$	56.5 cm | d = 10 mm, $\pi = 3.14$
31.4 mm | d = 12 m, $\pi = 3.14$	37.7 m | d = 23 mm, $\pi = 3.14$	72.3 mm | r = 2 m, $\pi = 3.14$
12.6 m | d = 24 m, $\pi = 3.14$	75.4 m | r = 15 mm, $\pi = 3.14$	94 mm | d = 15 cm, $\pi = 3.14$
47 cm | r = 0.5 m, $\pi = 3.14$	3.14 m | r = 1 cm, $\pi = 3.14$	6.28 cm | d = 20 cm, $\pi = 3.14$

72 inches (")	24 inches (")	2 feet (ft)	3 feet (ft)	36 inches (")	9 feet (ft)
108 inches (")	7040 yards (yds)	4 miles	72 inches (")	6 feet (ft)	54 inches (")
1 ½ yards (yds)	3 miles	5280 yards (yds)	4 feet (ft)	48 inches (")	½ mile
880 yards (yds)	324 inches (")	¾ yards (yds)	1760 yards (yds)	1 mile	5 ½ feet (ft)
66 inches (")	12 inches (")	1/3 yards (yds)	5 miles	8800 yards (yds)	¾ foot (ft)
9 inches (")	1 foot (ft)	12 inches (")	2½ miles	4400 yards (yds)	2 yards (yds)

8 pints	10 fluid ounces	½ pint	36 fluid ounces	1.8 pints	5 gallon
40 pints	6 gallon	48 pints	100 fluid ounces	5 pints	8 gallon
64 pints	6 fluid ounces	0.3 pint	1 pint	20 fluid ounces	9 gallon
72 pints	60 fluid ounces	3 pints	3 gallon	24 pints	2 fluid ounces
0.1 pints	8 fluid ounces	0.4 pint	½ gallon	4 pints	15 fluid ounces
¾ pint	¾ gallon	6 pints	40 fluid ounces	2 pints	1 gallon

7 pounds (lbs)	48 ounces (oz)
3 pounds (lbs)	126 pounds (lbs)
9 stone (st)	8 ounces (oz)
½ pounds (lbs)	10 stone (st)
140 pounds (lbs)	16 ounces (oz)
1 pound (lbs)	4 stone (st)
56 pounds (lbs)	80 ounces (oz)
5 pounds (lbs)	12 ounces (oz)
¾ pounds (lbs)	15 stone (st)
210 pounds (lbs)	14 pounds (lbs)
1 stone (st)	98 pounds (lbs)
7 stone (st)	100 ounces (oz)
6¼ pounds (lbs)	5 stone (st)
70 pounds (lbs)	240 ounces (oz)
15 pounds (lbs)	160 ounces (oz)
10 pounds (lbs)	128 ounces (oz)
8 pounds (lbs)	12 stone (st)
168 pounds (lbs)	112 ounces (oz)

8 km	20 fl. oz	1 pint	1 metre	1 yard	2.2 lbs
1 kg	18 litres	4 gallons	1 gallon	8 pints	1 stone
6 kg	1 oz	30 grams	1.6 km	1 mile	2 inches
5 cm	4½ litres	1 gallon	60 fl. oz	3 pints	100 fl. oz
5 pints	1¾ pints	1 litre	10 inches	25 cm	300 mm
12 inches	80 km	50 miles	200 grams	$6.6\dot{6}$ oz	5 miles

3.51 + 9.04	7.53	7.92 - 0.39	0.77	3.61 - 2.84	3.41
8.47 - 5.06	9.51	7.64 + 1.87	1.39	1.95 - 0.56	12.85
7.47 + 5.38	6.75	11.62 - 4.87	14.79	6.35 + 8.44	3.22
10.03 - 6.81	12.85	4.12 + 8.73	2.23	8.32 - 6.09	9.82
6.57 + 3.25	6.23	2.49 + 3.74	2.33	8.91 - 6.58	1.67
6.13 - 4.46	10.21	0.59 + 9.62	13.58	5.32 + 8.26	12.55

9	30 ÷ 0.2	150	20 ÷ 0.05	400	6 ÷ 0.4
15	700 ÷ 0.008	87500	9 ÷ 0.03	300	14 ÷ 0.007
2000	5 ÷ 0.001	5000	41 ÷ 0.02	2050	3 ÷ 0.006
500	2 ÷ 0.04	50	6 ÷ 0.2	30	32 ÷ 0.008
4000	80 ÷ 0.4	200	66 ÷ 0.03	2200	9 ÷ 0.5
18	7 ÷ 0.004	1750	56 ÷ 0.7	80	17 ÷ 0.02
850	24 ÷ 0.04	600	8 ÷ 0.005	1600	0.9 ÷ 0.1

0.06	7 x 0.5	3.5	60 x 0.03	1.8	140 x 0.4
56	23 x 0.1	2.3	8 x 0.006	0.048	90 x 0.5
45	500 x 0.07	35	4000 x 0.9	3600	700 x 0.5
350	80 x 0.6	48	140 x 0.004	0.56	30 x 0.02
0.6	70 x 0.3	21	600 x 0.09	54	40 x 0.009
0.36	14 x 0.4	5.6	80 x 0.006	0.48	40 x 0.09
3.6	12 x 0.005	0.06	9000 x 0.09	810	30 x 0.002

-3 + 2	2
-7 + 9	1
-2 +3	-20
-11 +-9	-5
-2 +-3	-2
7 + -9	-2
-11 + 9	3
-5 + 8	2
11 +-9	-13
-5 + -8	-28
-10 + -18	-8
10 + -18	8
-10 + 18	-15
-9 + -6	-3
5 + -8	-15
-8 + -7	5
-4 + 9	6
9 + -3	-1

24 | $-10 \div -2$	5 | -3×2	-6 | $-28 \div 7$
-4 | -8×-6	48 | $-50 \div -5$	10 | 3×-8
-24 | $-72 \div 12$	-6 | $-60 \div -12$	5 | -3×-2
6 | 5×-2	-10 | -6×-7	42 | $-36 \div -9$
4 | $63 \div -7$	-9 | -9×8	-72 | $-27 \div 3$
-9 | 7×-8	-56 | $40 \div -8$	-5 | -4×-6

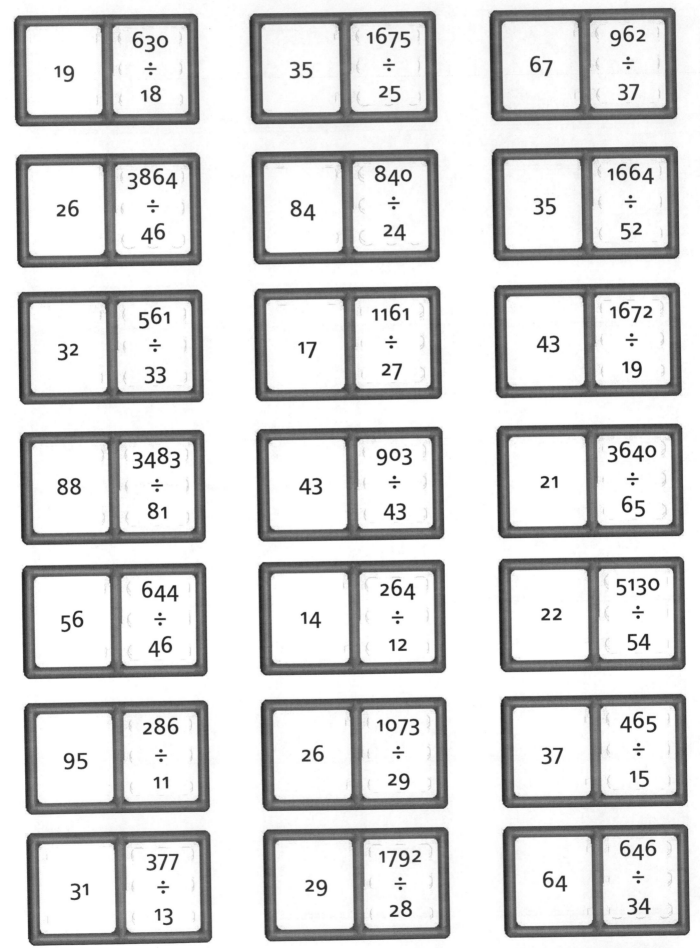

19	630 ÷ 18	35	1675 ÷ 25	67	962 ÷ 37
26	3864 ÷ 46	84	840 ÷ 24	35	1664 ÷ 52
32	561 ÷ 33	17	1161 ÷ 27	43	1672 ÷ 19
88	3483 ÷ 81	43	903 ÷ 43	21	3640 ÷ 65
56	644 ÷ 46	14	264 ÷ 12	22	5130 ÷ 54
95	286 ÷ 11	26	1073 ÷ 29	37	465 ÷ 15
31	377 ÷ 13	29	1792 ÷ 28	64	646 ÷ 34

81	2.67×78.4
240	$93.6 \div 2.3$
45	$\frac{320.1 \times 19.4}{0.89}$
6000	$\frac{36.45 \times 4.98}{2.37}$
100	4.6^2
25	23.09×112.98
2300	0.67×22.9
14	$290.7 \div 63.4$
5	$\frac{94.721 \times 32.1}{47.2}$
50	$\frac{8021 \times 2.3}{3.798}$
4000	7.3^2
49	35.72×0.33
12	$237.35 \div 42.68$
6	$\sqrt{78.35}$
9	$319.54 \div 78.2$
4	$871.6 \div 9.72$
90	12.598×0.2469
3	9.25^2

Gradient of -1	$Y = 3X + 2$
Gradient of 3 Intercept of 2	$Y = 2X + 3$
Gradient of 2 Intercept of 3	$Y = 5X + 4$
Gradient of 5 Intercept of 4	$Y = 4X - 5$
Gradient of 4 Intercept of -5	$Y = 2X + 4$
Gradient of 2 Intercept of (0,4)	$Y = 3X - 5$
Gradient of 3 Intercept of (0,-5)	$Y = -2X + 4$
Gradient of -2 Intercept of (0,4)	$Y = -2X + 4$
Gradient of -2 Intercept of (0,-4)	$Y = \frac{1}{2}X + 4$
Gradient of ½ Intercept of (0,4)	$Y = \frac{1}{2}X - 5$
Gradient of ½ Intercept of (0,-5)	$Y = -3X + 2$
Gradient of -3 Intercept of 2	$Y = -2X + 3$
Gradient of -2 Intercept of 3	$Y = \frac{1}{8}X - 1$
Gradient of $\frac{1}{8}$ Intercept of (0,-1)	$Y = -\frac{1}{2}X + 6$
Gradient of $-\frac{1}{2}$ Intercept of 6	$Y = X - \frac{1}{8}$
Gradient of 1 Intercept of $(0,-\frac{1}{8})$	$Y = -X - 2$
Gradient of -1 Intercept of (0,-2)	$Y = -4X - \frac{3}{4}$
Gradient of-4 Intercept of $-\frac{3}{4}$	$Y = -X$

$2x = 6$	4
$7x = 56$	10
$8x = 16$	5
$4x = 24$	12
$6x = 42$	9
$10x = 75$	11
$3x = 12$	8
$9x = 90$	2
$12x = 60$	6
$2x = 24$	7
$5x = 45$	$7\frac{1}{2}$
$3x = 33$	3

11	$x + 3 = 11$	8	$x - 7 = 23$	30	$x + 6 = 8$
2	$x + 9 = 26$	17	$x + 20 = 16$	-4	$x - 6 = 18$
24	$x - 9 = 7$	16	$x - 3 = 11$	14	$x + 10 = 7$
-3	$x - 6 = -8$	-2	$x + 9 = 27$	18	$x - 2 = -11$
-9	$x - 8 = 7$	15	$x + 9 = 21$	12	$x - 12 = 24$
36	$x - 11 = -3$	8	$x + 5 = 6$	1	$x + 3 = -11$
-14	$x + 10 = 5$	-5	$x + 23 = 22$	-1	$x - 7 = 4$

$2X + 1 = 19$	2.5 ($2\frac{1}{2}$)
$5X - 7 = 8$	8
$7X - 9 = 40$	2
$9X - 2 = 43$	4
$8X - 1 = 79$	6
$3X + 2 = 2$	12

$3X + 4 = 28$	9
$9X + 12 = 30$	3
$6X + 3 = 27$	7
$4X + 8 = 56$	5
$2X - 5 = 19$	10
$6X + 1 = 16$	0

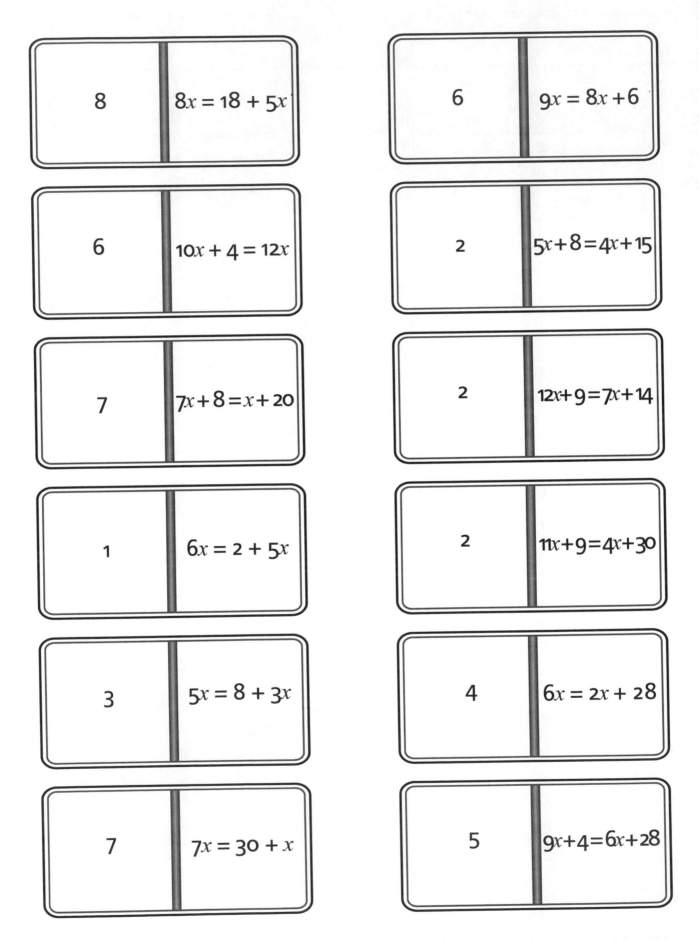

8	$8x = 18 + 5x$	6	$9x = 8x + 6$
6	$10x + 4 = 12x$	2	$5x + 8 = 4x + 15$
7	$7x + 8 = x + 20$	2	$12x + 9 = 7x + 14$
1	$6x = 2 + 5x$	2	$11x + 9 = 4x + 30$
3	$5x = 8 + 3x$	4	$6x = 2x + 28$
7	$7x = 30 + x$	5	$9x + 4 = 6x + 28$

144	$\frac{7}{8}$ of 776	679	$\frac{3}{4}$ of 144	108	$\frac{5}{6}$ of 564
470	$\frac{2}{3}$ of 135	90	$\frac{2}{5}$ of 125	50	$\frac{3}{11}$ of 253
69	$\frac{5}{9}$ of 243	135	$\frac{2}{7}$ of 273	78	$\frac{5}{8}$ of 152
95	$\frac{5}{12}$ of 420	175	$\frac{6}{13}$ of 507	234	$\frac{7}{9}$ of 261
203	$\frac{7}{10}$ of 450	315	$\frac{9}{11}$ of 231	189	$\frac{4}{9}$ of 306
136	$\frac{3}{8}$ of 136	51	$\frac{5}{12}$ of 444	185	$\frac{2}{9}$ of 648

$3\frac{5}{6}$	$\frac{3}{2}$	$1\frac{1}{2}$	$\frac{9}{4}$	$2\frac{1}{4}$	$\frac{11}{5}$
$2\frac{1}{5}$	$\frac{17}{3}$	$5\frac{2}{3}$	$\frac{73}{10}$	$7\frac{3}{10}$	$\frac{31}{6}$
$5\frac{1}{6}$	$\frac{11}{3}$	$3\frac{2}{3}$	$\frac{13}{2}$	$6\frac{1}{2}$	$\frac{23}{5}$
$4\frac{3}{5}$	$\frac{31}{3}$	$10\frac{1}{3}$	$\frac{41}{7}$	$5\frac{6}{7}$	$\frac{19}{6}$
$3\frac{1}{6}$	$\frac{35}{11}$	$3\frac{2}{11}$	$\frac{91}{9}$	$10\frac{1}{9}$	$\frac{27}{8}$
$3\frac{3}{8}$	$\frac{23}{4}$	$5\frac{3}{4}$	$\frac{25}{10}$	$2\frac{1}{2}$	$\frac{23}{6}$

12 x 34	1675	25 x 67	990	45 x 22	1887
37 x 51	4960	62 x 80	4307	59 x 73	325
13 x 25	3124	71 x 44	2565	95 x 27	5616
78 x 72	3510	54 x 65	1645	35 x 47	476
17 x 28	592	37 x 16	3410	62 x 55	4464
48 x 93	1633	23 x 71	2816	88 x 32	408

None	7
Prime	25
Square	14
None	2
Prime	8
Cube	36
Square	64
Square and Cube	23
Prime	27
Cube	49
Square	5
Prime	18

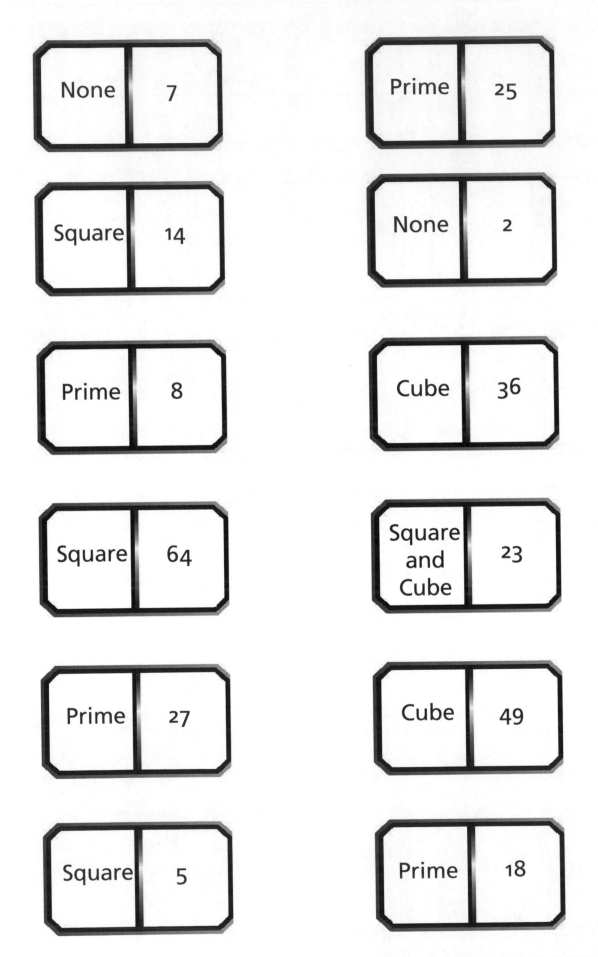

44.02	12% of 40	4.8	63% of 60	37.8	41% of 24
9.84	78% of 55	42.9	26% of 34	8.84	32% of 75
24	16% of 44	7.04	55% of 68	37.4	27% of 82
22.14	9% of 17	1.53	22% of 36	7.92	65% of 134
87.1	43% of 29	12.47	86% of 210	180.6	6% of 78
4.68	92% of 42	38.64	33% of 39	12.87	71% of 62

$\frac{3}{4}$	Probability of a coin landing on HEADS.
$\frac{1}{2}$	P (**red**) from a bag of counters with **3 red** and **5 blue** counters.
$\frac{3}{8}$	Prob (Letter **M**) in the word **IMAGINATION.**
$\frac{1}{11}$	Prob (number< 2) on a fair 6 sided dice.
$\frac{1}{6}$	Probability of an ODD number on a fair 6 sided dice.
$\frac{1}{2}$	P (**green**) from a bag of counters with **3 red** and **5 blue** counters.
0	Probability of a blue sock from a drawer of 15 socks – where 4 are blue.
$\frac{4}{15}$	P (**counter**) from a bag of counters with **3 red** and **5 blue** counters.
1	Prob (Letter I) in the word IMAGINATION
$\frac{3}{11}$	Prob (Letter L) in the word CHALLENGING
$\frac{2}{11}$	Prob (number> 5) on a fair 6 sided dice.
$\frac{1}{6}$	P (**purple**) in a pencil case of **5 reds, 6 blues** and **4 purples.**
$\frac{4}{15}$	P (**red**) in a pencil case of **5 reds, 6 blues** and **4 purples.**
$\frac{1}{3}$	Prob (**WIN**) if you bought **50** tickets from a raffle that sold **200** tickets.
$\frac{1}{4}$	P (**blue**) from a bag of counters with **3 red** and **5 blue** counters.
$\frac{5}{8}$	Prob (**VOWEL**) in the word **IMAGINATION.**
$\frac{6}{11}$	P (**blue**) in a pencil case of **5 reds, 6 blues** and **4 purples.**
$\frac{2}{5}$	Prob (**LOSE**) if you bought **50** tickets from a raffle that sold **200** tickets.

3:8	16:18	8:9	24:8	3:1	20:15
4:3	99:18	11:2	27:12	9:4	45:40
9:8	36:20	9:5	12:18	2:3	28:35
4:5	21:18	7:6	45:36	5:4	72:48
3:2	9:15	3:5	72:18	4:1	32:20
8:5	22:99	2:9	27:63	3:7	18:48

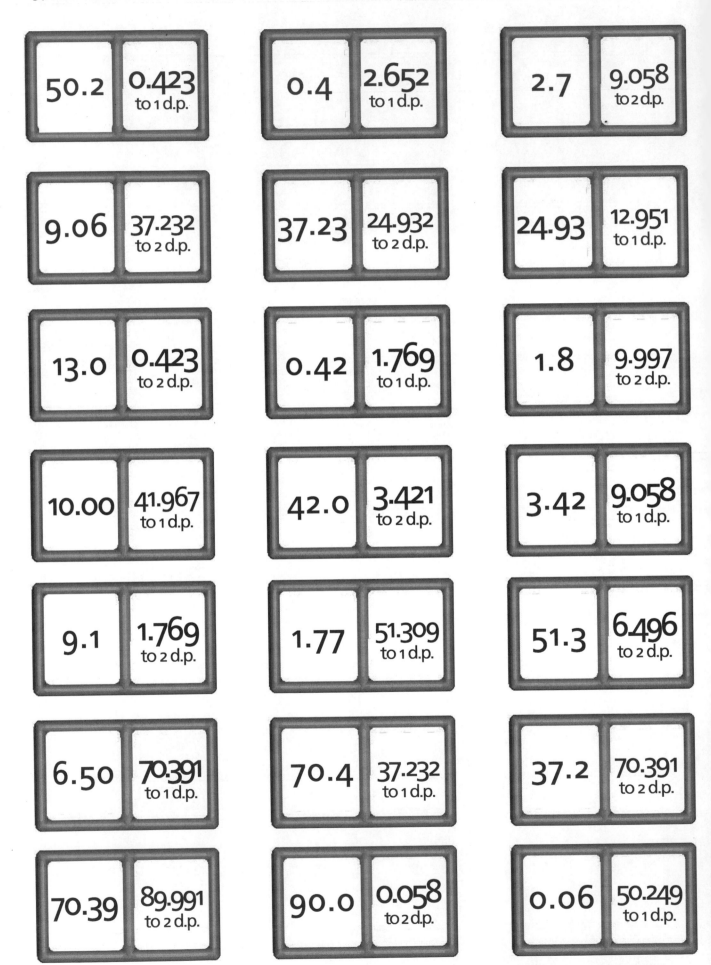

50.2	0.423 to 1 d.p.	0.4	2.652 to 1 d.p.	2.7	9.058 to 2 d.p.
9.06	37.232 to 2 d.p.	37.23	24.932 to 2 d.p.	24.93	12.951 to 1 d.p.
13.0	0.423 to 2 d.p.	0.42	1.769 to 1 d.p.	1.8	9.997 to 2 d.p.
10.00	41.967 to 1 d.p.	42.0	3.421 to 2 d.p.	3.42	9.058 to 1 d.p.
9.1	1.769 to 2 d.p.	1.77	51.309 to 1 d.p.	51.3	6.496 to 2 d.p.
6.50	70.391 to 1 d.p.	70.4	37.232 to 1 d.p.	37.2	70.391 to 2 d.p.
70.39	89.991 to 2 d.p.	90.0	0.058 to 2 d.p.	0.06	50.249 to 1 d.p.

$5a + 8b$	$3a + 5a$	$8a$	$12a + 3b + 4a$	$16a + 3b$	$3b + 5a + 2b$
$5a + 5b$	$7a + 5a$	$12a$	$4b + b$	$5b$	$2a + 3a - 4a + 5b$
$a + 5b$	$2b + 6a - b - 3a$	$3a + b$	$-7a + 2b - 3a + 4b + 5a$	$-5a + 6b$	$3b + 4b - a + 6b + 11a$
$10a + 13b$	$-2a + 4b + 5a + 5b - 3a$	$9b$	$2a + 6b - 5a$	$-3a + 6b$	$2b - a + 7a - 3b + 7b + 5a + 4a$
$15a + 6b$	$7a + 2b + 8a - b - 2a - b$	$13a$	$7a + 3b + a + 6b + 2a$	$10a + 9b$	$4b + 9a - 3b - 6a + 3a$
$6a + b$	$8a - 2b + 7b - 2a + 5b$	$6a + 10b$	$4b + 9a - 2b - 6a$	$3a + 2b$	$6a + 3b - a$
$5a + 3b$	$6b - 5a + b - 3a$	$-8a + 7b$	$2a + 7b - a - b$	$a + 6b$	$8b + 3a + 2a$

789 - 45	191	264 - 73	308	395 - 87	144
198 - 54	241	302 - 61	167	189 - 22	405
483 - 78	431	526 - 95	783	827 - 44	639
692 - 63	43	109 - 66	287	371 - 84	415
449 - 34	312	399 - 87	475	527 - 52	778
841 - 63	199	290 - 91	959	987 - 28	744

$0.83\dot{3}$ hours	45 mins	0.75 hours	20 mins	$0.3\dot{3}$ hours	30 mins
0.5 hours	16 mins	$0.26\dot{6}$ hours	24 mins	0.4 hours	54 mins
0.9 hours	72 mins	1.2 hours	15 mins	0.25 hours	105 mins
1.75 hours	42 mins	0.7 hours	6 mins	0.1 hours	95 mins
$1.58\dot{3}$ hours	90 mins	1.5 hours	36 mins	0.6 hours	222 mins
3.7 hours	10 mins	$0.16\dot{6}$ hours	120 mins	2 hours	50 mins

288 mm^3

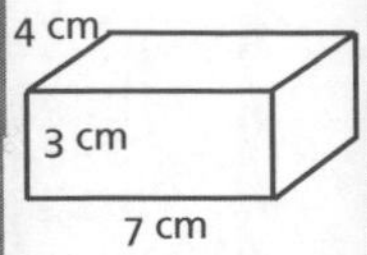

216 cm^3

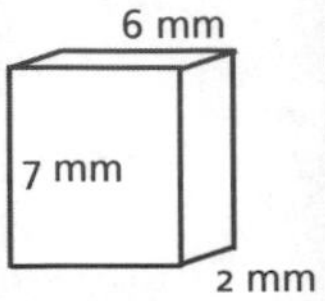

80 cm^3

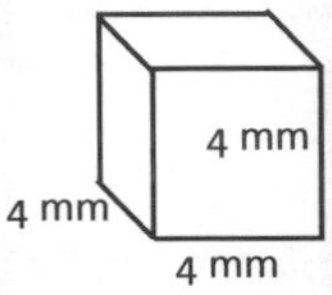

240 cm^3

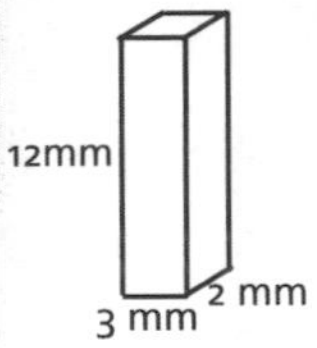

168 cm^3

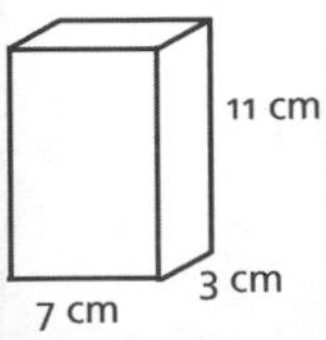

144 cm^3

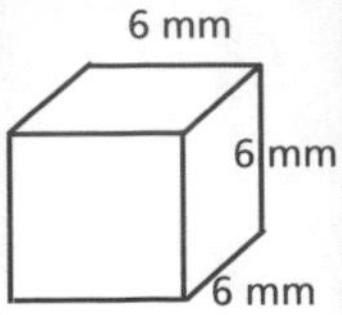

84 cm^3

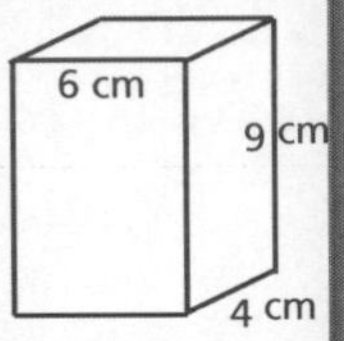

84 mm^3

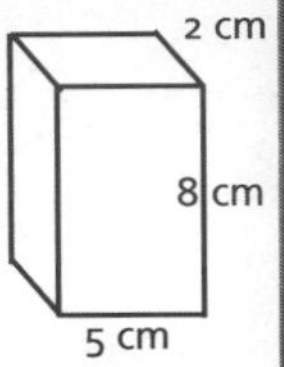

64 mm^3

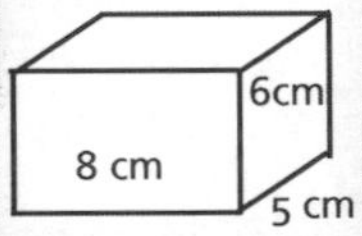

72 mm^3

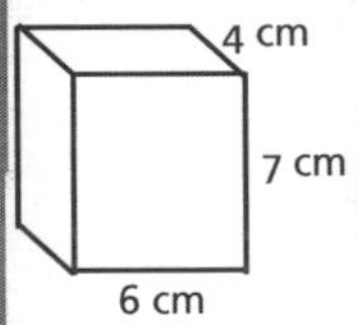

231 cm^3

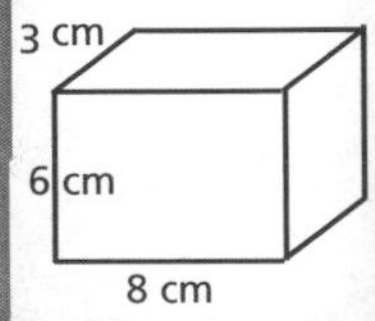

216 mm^3

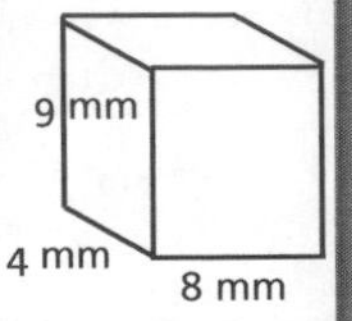

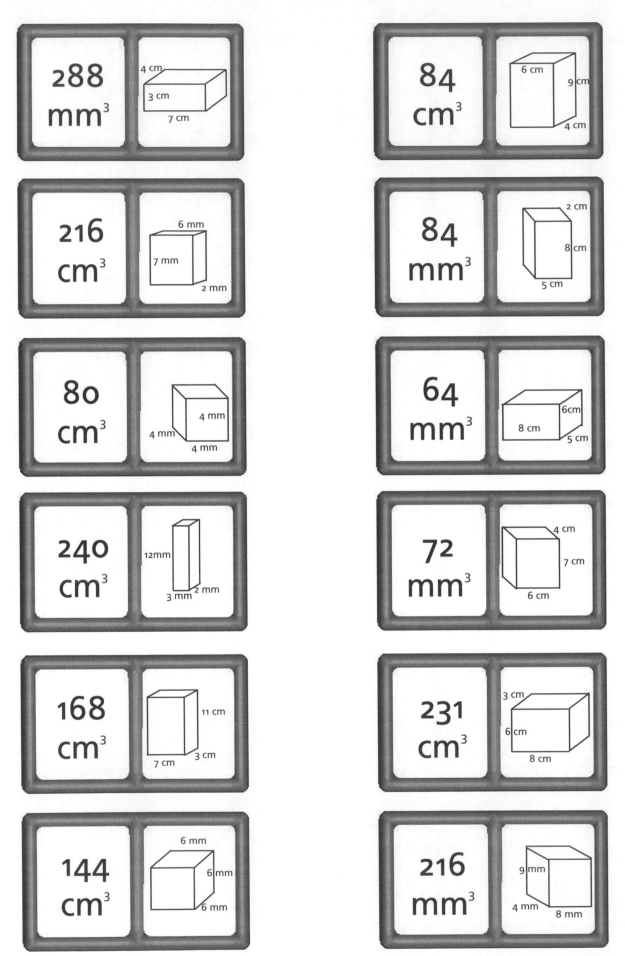

39. Mathematical Dominoes 1 - 12 Domino Template

40. Mathematical Dominoes 1 - 18 Domino Template

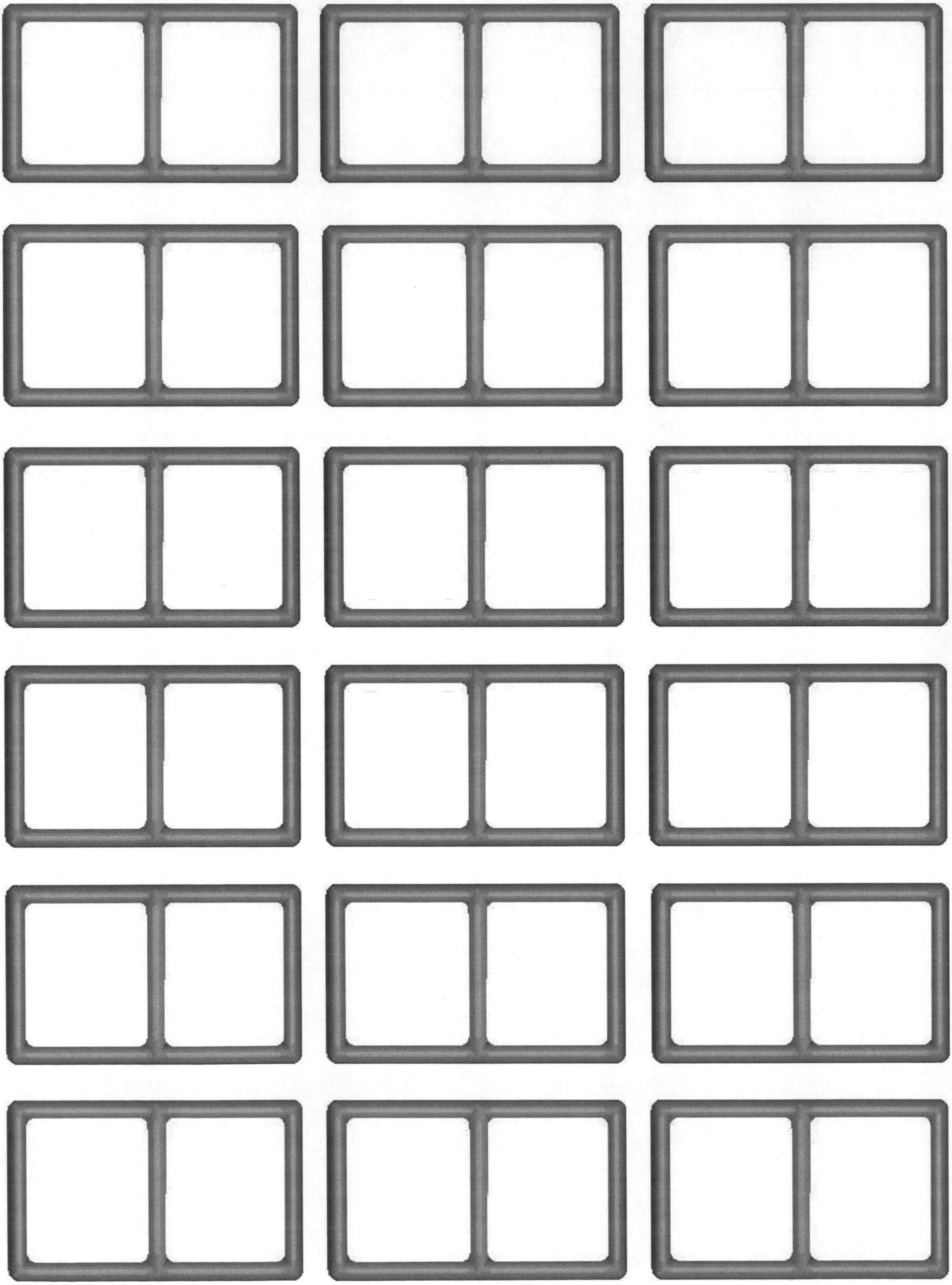